Ghost Stories:
The Carrier Bag Theory of Architecture

Türkiye Pavilion
18th International Architecture Exhibition
La Biennale di Venezia

Curators: Sevince Bayrak, Oral Göktaş

La Biennale di Venezia

18. Mostra
Internazionale
di Architettura

Partecipazioni Nazionali

AF194537

ISTANBUL
FOUNDATION
FOR CULTURE
AND ARTS

LISTLAB

GHOST STORIES:
The Carrier Bag Theory
of Architecture

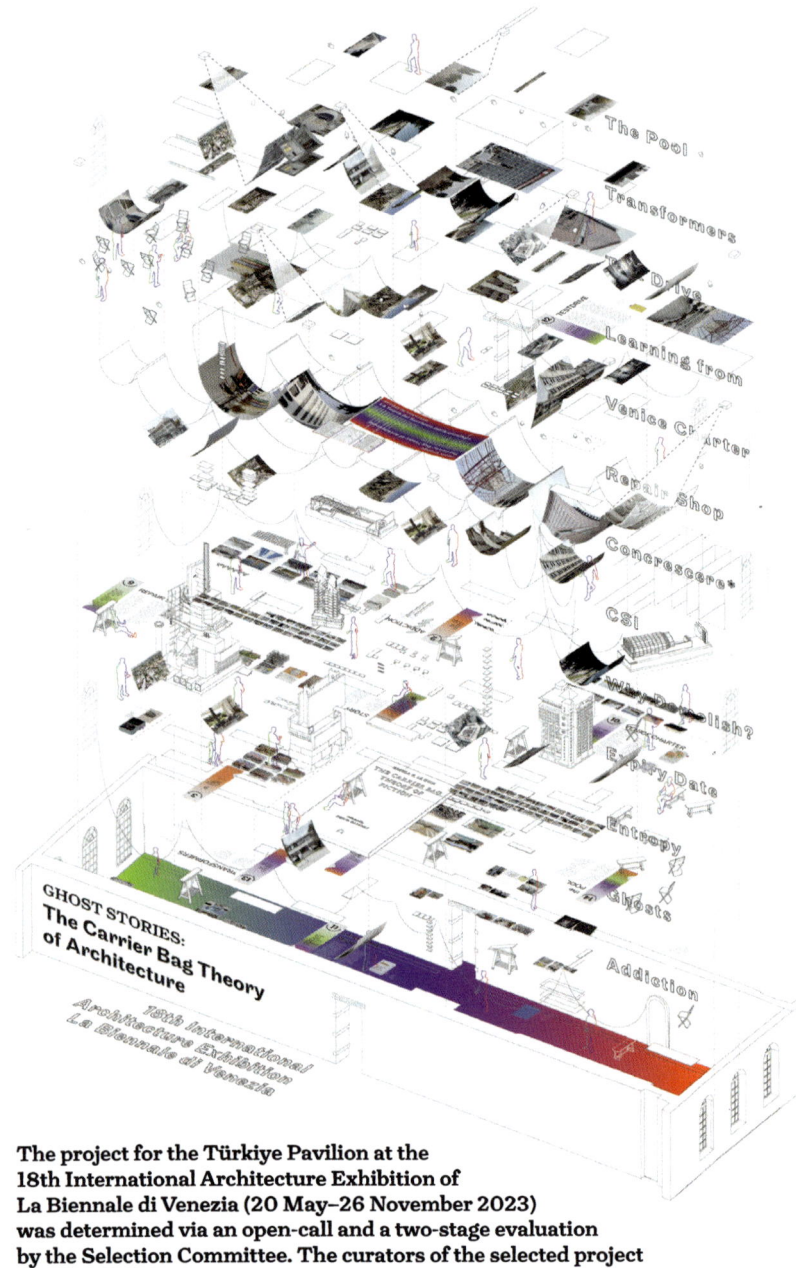

The Pool

Transformers

Drive

Learning from

Venice Charter

Repair Shop

Concrescere*

CSI

Why Demolish?

Expiry Date

Entropy

Ghosts

Addiction

GHOST STORIES:
The Carrier Bag Theory
of Architecture

18th International
Architecture Exhibition
La Biennale di Venezia

The project for the Türkiye Pavilion at the
18th International Architecture Exhibition of
La Biennale di Venezia (20 May–26 November 2023)
was determined via an open-call and a two-stage evaluation
by the Selection Committee. The curators of the selected project
– *Ghost Stories: The Carrier Bag Theory of Architecture* –
are Sevince Bayrak and Oral Göktaş.

INTRODUCTION

As the Istanbul Foundation for Culture and Arts (İKSV), we are delighted to work with Sevince Bayrak and Oral Göktaş as the curators of the Türkiye Pavilion at the 18th International Architecture Exhibition of La Biennale di Venezia. *Ghost Stories: The Carrier Bag Theory of Architecture* brings a fresh perspective to the field of architecture by proposing a shift in its focus to the utilisation of tremendous unused building stock.

Our curators have adopted an engaging, collective research method and launched an open call on social media for people to report abandoned buildings, receiving extensive documentation across Türkiye. Can unused buildings with different functions become a 'laboratory of the future' and be transformed instead of being demolished? Can a new architectural understanding define the building as a container that holds people together? Can architecture pay attention to the stories of abandoned buildings? All of these questions and potential solutions were brought together in 'A Manifesto for *The Carrier Bag Theory of Architecture*' that laid the ground for the exhibition.

This central issue of the exhibition became even more urgent after one of the most catastrophic natural disasters of the last few decades struck Southeastern Türkiye and Northern Syria. On 6 February, 7.8 and 7.6 magnitude earthquakes were felt from 460 km away and devastated the entire region. This is a critical moment to find different forms of solidarity and think of new methods and strategies to transform existing structures.

I am grateful to Sevince Bayrak and Oral Göktaş for meticulously curating this edition and presenting hopeful solutions to imagine an alternative future. I also thank Selen Erkal, Duygu Şengünler and Aslı Kocamaz, who, along with myself, are the core members of the Türkiye Pavilion. Our graphic designer Esen Karol, our editorial manager Erim Şerifoğlu, the project team, the research team and the İKSV teams have also worked on this project with precision and care.

I would like to thank the Republic of Türkiye Ministry of Culture and Tourism and the Ministry of Foreign Affairs who give their invaluable support to the pavilion as always; our principal sponsors Schüco Turkey and VitrA, and the airline partner, Turkish Airlines.

BİGE ÖRER
Director of İKSV Contemporary Art Projects

Abandoned swimming pool at Istanbul Planning Agency (IPA) Campus

GHOST STORIES:
The Carrier Bag Theory of Architecture

STORY

An abandoned swimming pool, lined with out-dated
blue mosaic tiles, where only seagulls float. Surrounded
by pine trees, the empty swimming pool is hidden away
in the middle of the forest. When the gaudy yellow
roof structure opens up, the surface of the pool meets
the sky. Though neglected, the pool holds stories.

THEORY

Elizabeth Fisher argues that, rather than hunting tools,
the first cultural device used by humans was probably
a carrier bag, which allowed them to transport the
vegetables they gathered.[1] A weapon-wielding man,
however, is apparently a more captivating image to
depict on the walls of a cave than a food-carrying scene.

Fisher's 'Carrier Bag Theory of Evolution' not only
restructures the story of humanity from a different
perspective, but the theory itself opens up space for
those who come after her to develop new theories
about cultural production. The adoption of carrier
bag theories, whether in fiction or architecture, brings
a radical change to the images we have inherited
through the paintings on the walls of prehistoric caves,
through stories or through the modern cityscape.
When these images start to change, a shift in our
way of doing things is required. Thus moving from
the image of a weapon to a carrier bag eventually
transforms the whole scene from a heroic, legendary

---

1   Elizabeth Fisher, *Woman's Creation: Sexual Evolution and the Shaping
of Society* (New York: Anchor Press, 1979), pp. 56–61.

story of destruction to a collaborative, unfamiliar life story. Heroes and hunting scenes no longer dominate the story. Instead, the story focuses on collaborative actions such as observing and collecting existing things, sharing them, and transforming them as necessary.

Ursula K. Le Guin adapted Fisher's theory to fiction, and used it to tell gripping stories in which unheroic characters make their way through life, with all its failures and conflicts. *The Carrier Bag Theory of Architecture* applies Le Guin's theory to architectural practice. In our age of crisis, a fundamental change in architecture is required. As architects, can we tolerate such a radical rethinking of the images we have inherited, our ossified perceptions of beauty and functionality? What if we listen to and understand the stories of abandoned buildings, rather than focusing on more heroic, successful examples?

Hunting scene in Çatalhöyük, 6000 B.C. People wielding bows and arrows to hunt wild boar and deer

The world's oldest woven basket, found in Muraba'at Cave in 2021, preserved for 10,500 years thanks to the dry climate

Adapting the carrier bag theory to architecture recalls the fundamentals of architecture, reminding us of the primary reason why we need spaces that hold, protect and cherish us, and how we make them. *The Carrier Bag Theory of Architecture* is based on transforming existing structures. Whatever exists in the scene, human or non-human, material or immaterial, becomes the subject of this theory. In fact, the theory extends back to the time when hominids first started building. For ages, human beings have been building with/onto existing materials. Early hominids lived in close relationship with the landscape, thinking about ways to transform what they found into the tools they needed. Materials in their habitat were diverse: hair, vines and hides[2] were

2   Ibid.

easily transformed into bags to carry or nests in which to rest. The container, whether a net made of human hair, a basket made of wild oats, or even a home, was created from whatever existed in their surroundings.[3]

If we define a building as a container, as a carrier bag, or as a pool that holds a life story of transformations, unpredictability and messiness, then the building becomes the site itself and architecture no longer needs empty plots in order to flourish, but existing structures to begin the transformation.

Building as a carrier bag that contains stories

3   Ursula K. Le Guin, *The Carrier Bag Theory of Fiction* (Birmingham UK: Terra Ignota, 2019), p. 32.

We looked at the big hole covered with little blue tiles. We could put in some steps, maybe add a platform to sit on, and anchor some plates onto the yellow roof structure so that it can absorb the sound of the inhabitants. This story cannot compete with the one where the Hero struggles with the topography, challenges gravity and stands tall as a structure to be seen, covered with precious materials that have been carved out from miles away to achieve a spectacle at great expense. In the latter story, the constantly pumping adrenalin becomes addictive, just like the act of construction itself ...

ADDICTION

...since construction is not a productive field, its contribution to production is limited, and therefore it must be produced continuously for production increase. This results in a kind of 'narcotic effect' that becomes addictive to politicians. Construction addiction, like any addiction, tends to 'focus on the moment', narrows the time horizon and evaporates the ability to think about the future.[4] — ENSAR YILMAZ

The ability to think about the future might have been what prompted early hominids to design a carrier bag. In order not to have to gather plants in bad weather, they needed a bag to carry more food than they could immediately consume.[5]

4   Ensar Yılmaz, 'İnşaatın politik ekonomisi: İnşaat sadece inşaat değildir' [The political economy of construction: Construction is never just construction], *Gazete Duvar*, 7 December 2020, gazeteduvar.com.tr/insaatin-politik-ekonomisi-insaat-sadece-insaat-degildir-haber-1506458. Author's translation.

5   Le Guin, op. cit. p. 28.

When the ability to think about the future no longer exists, buildings do not need a particular reason to be constructed. It is the construction addiction rather than spatial needs that causes a building to exist. This addiction creates a construction boom – a period of rapid development of new buildings. The phenomenon has been observed in various countries around the world, including China, the UK and US. Like a shopping addict's wardrobe stuffed with unnecessary items, cities are filled with disused buildings and useless infrastructure.

Türkiye has suffered from this addiction as well. Passing through a period of development fuelled mainly by construction, the country has ended up with numerous unsold real-estate projects ranging from housing to transportation. In 2019, *Dezeen*, a renowned design magazine, featured a Turkish project on its cover as it announced the most significant architecture and design news of the year.[6] The news from Türkiye was about an abandoned real-estate project called Burj Al Babas, which was planned to contain 732 identical mini chateaux when finished. However, the contractors failed to sell the 587 villas that were completed, and went bankrupt. Although the architects claimed that they developed the design of the villas based on the desires and demands of customers, who were mostly from Gulf countries,[7] no-one was willing to live in this brand new village

6   Tom Ravenscroft, 'The Biggest Architecture and Design Stories of 2019', *Dezeen*, 6 January 2020, dezeen.com/2019/12/31/biggest-architecture-design-stories-2019.

7   'Bolu'da Araplar İçin İnşa Edilen "Şatolar" Elde Kaldı' [The 'Castles' Built for the Arabs in Bolu Remained Unsold], *DW Türkçe*, 9 January 2019. youtube.com/watch?v=2ROMXecYPoE.

packed with identical houses. Burj Al Babas has become a symbol of construction addiction and an inability to think about the future, resulting in an economic failure as well as an urban one.

In the revised edition of the classic book *The Limits to Growth*, the authors propose that as long as society lacks better solutions, 'it will never let go of its addiction to growth, because people so badly need hope'. They conclude that 'growth may be a false hope, but it is better than no hope at all'.[1] However, in the case of Burj Al Babas, it was not society that was in desperate need of hope, but the construction market, which was badly hit during the economic crisis of 2018.

[1]   Donella H. Meadows, Dennis L. Meadows and Jørgen Randers, *Limits to Growth: The 30-Year Update* (Falls Church, VA: Potomac Associates, 2004), p. 261.

**Ghost Stories from different cities in Türkiye that
were collected through an open call in 2023**

GHOSTS

...all stories are, more or less,
ghost stories.[8] — JULIAN WOLFREYS

The Carrier Bag Theory of Architecture begins with revealing the story of neglected buildings. Surrounded by life, these buildings are almost invisible. They are decrepit ghosts that are not even capable of scaring people. But once they are uncovered and pulled on stage, they change the whole scenography.

Existing buildings are just like ancient sites – they can provide a foundation for the next one to be built upon. If abandoned, they can become the new landscape from which the architecture rises. While, for real-estate developers, it is impossible to ignore an empty plot in a city, an abandoned building can be neglected for years. Only when architecture accepts abandoned buildings as a site to transform, can this systematic act of neglect be diminished.

What do these abandoned buildings tell us? Why do we need to listen to, understand and speak with them? They will help us comprehend what we have inherited. Conversations with ghosts do not necessarily aim to uncover hidden or embarrassing information. Instead, they can bring about an understanding of the concept of secrecy itself, which involves a fundamental lack of knowledge that may challenge or disrupt what we think we know.[9]

8   Julian Wolfreys, *Victorian Hauntings: Spectrality, Gothic, the Uncanny and Literature* (London: Bloomsbury Publishing, 2017), p. 3.

9   Colin J. Davis, 'Hauntology, Spectres and Phantoms', *French Studies* 59, no. 3 (1 July 2005): 373–79.

Full of conflicts and failures, ghosts can't be heroes, but they can carry stories through walls.

A series of ghosts accompanies us as we drive along the highway. Dinosaurs, roller coasters, towers, transformer robots... The whole scene looks like a psychedelic nightmare. Ankapark in Ankara, the largest theme park in Europe, was opened in Atatürk Forest Farm in 2019. However, it was abandoned just a few months after opening for technical, legal and financial reasons. There were seventeen roller coasters built on the ground – an infertile swamp that had been reported to be inappropriate for such a massive construction. That is why it was chosen as an area to rehabilitate in 1925, to constitute the Atatürk Forest Farm, one of the first human-made recreation areas of the newly found Republic.[10] The haunted site, the size of 120 football fields, now sits in the middle of the capital, Ankara, waiting for a new purpose.

In the case of Ankapark, ghost stories become entangled. From addiction to construction to immense corruption and discussions of identity politics, the stories reveal the complex web of factors that contributed to the destruction of the Forest Farm, as well as the subsequent development of Ankapark. The theme park will remain closed until the municipality decides its future, together with the public. Until then, the most likely scenario seems to be that nature will reclaim the abandoned structures, most of which are already dilapidated.

---

10   Atatürk Orman Çiftliği [Atatürk Forest Farm], 'Tarihçe' [History], n.d., aoc.gov.tr/Portal/Kategorilcerik/tarihce/49.

Ankapark, Ankara, 2023

ENTROPY

> A building is made against entropy by our inputs of energy, and like a living thing, once it is made, it requires a constant input of energy to maintain itself against decay. That is how we keep buildings 'alive'. An abandoned building will not maintain itself. It will decay – a kind of analogous 'death' by increased disorder (entropy).[11] — MARK WEST

From the perspective of physics, existing structures are the rearranged molecules of the Earth that transit from one phase to another as they are transferred from one site to another. Even though construction might simply be defined as the transition and transportation of materials, modern methods of demolition interrupt the cycle, leaving rubble as a site-filling element, rather than a reusable material.

11 Mark West, interviewed by the author, 5 March 2022.

As Caitlin DeSilvey notes, 'the concepts of decay and entropy have the potential to be contradictory and can be interpreted as positive or negative, constructive or destructive, depending on the context'.[12]

Though transforming existing structures should be at the very centre of the construction industry rather than being a niche practice, the mainstream institutions currently neglect the power of transformation. The whole construction industry and its side sectors need fundamental and systematic change in order to let existing structures be considered as untapped resources rather than less-profitable operations.

Even though decarbonisation is a current trend in construction, in 2018, the biggest proportion of both worldwide final energy consumption (36%) and CO_2 emissions caused by energy usage (39%) was attributed to the construction and operation of buildings.[13] As Carl Elefante puts it, 'the greenest building is ... one that is already built'.[14]

It is clear that the construction industry needs to be reconfigured from scratch, rather than through partial solutions that endeavour to diminish carbon emission in specific phases of the construction process. If the end product of a construction project – which might either be a building or

12 Caitlin DeSilvey, *Curated Decay: Heritage beyond Saving* (Minneapolis: University of Minnesota Press, 2017), p. 12.

13 *Global Status Report for Buildings and Construction 2019* (Paris: IEA, 2019), p. 12.

14 Carl Elefante, "The Greenest Building Is ... One That Is Already Built" *Forum Journal* 21, 2007, no: 4 (Summer 2007): 26–38.

infrastructure – is not in use, this simply means that the energy consumed to achieve a building will not be able to evolve into the energy that generates relations between buildings, people and nature.

Existing buildings are the embodiment of how society, technology and investment – both economic and social – consolidate in the landscape. They present an overlap with the panorama of the period in which they were built, and the period through which they have survived. Existing structures offer an abundant resource of materials and memory that no longer require humans to constantly reshape the Earth.

Dosan Canned Food Facility, Bursa. Architect: Aydın Boysan

EXPIRY DATE

The nature of the product being sold, which is that of a durable good, creates a type of price stickiness for companies because it allows them to wait. Therefore, buildings can remain empty for years as supply exceeds demand for an extended period of time.[15] — ENSAR YILMAZ

Heroes have expiry dates. Buildings don't. Once designed to be the Hero of the neighbourhood, certain buildings become like forgotten Hollywood stars when they are abandoned. They are no longer Heroes but ordinary structures waiting to be rediscovered. There

Kahramanmaraş Special Provincial Administration, designed by Haldun Sunal and Arif Nafiz Aköz, built in 1994, expired in 2022

15   Yılmaz, op. cit.

are buildings that have never become Heroes throughout their lifetimes. They are either neglected, or merge so well into the existing cityscape that they become almost invisible.

Making a building is the result of a compromise for decision makers, land owners, clients, developers and users. When the compromise is no longer available, buildings expire.

Spolia

From the Latin spolium, *meaning booty or loot. In Turkish the term is devşirmek, which means to collect, to aggregate.*

> you-can't-just-cast-that-away-when-it-gets-inconvenient[16] — DONNA HARAWAY

It was once very common for people to utilise whatever existed in the landscape as a resource for their own purposes. Before construction became an industry that required the constant production of buildings or building components, existing material was utilised to speed up the building process. People who constructed ancient temples, colossal cisterns and giant forums reused the materials of previous structures from different civilisations. Though 'spolia', the word for repurposed building elements, coming from a Latin root that means 'booty' – the spoils of war

---

16 'Making Kin: An Interview with Donna Haraway', *Los Angeles Review of Books*, 6 December 2019, lareviewofbooks.org/article/making-kin-an-interview-with-donna-haraway.

– has a negative connotation, the Turkish word for this act of repurposing is *devşirme*, which means to collect, without any pejorative hint. During the times when construction was defined as an act of accumulating what was already there on site, people repurposed existing materials not only for monumental buildings but for any kind of structure necessary in daily life.

When *Hayat* magazine sent Ara Güler to photograph the opening of Kemer Dam in 1958, he lost his way on his return and spent the night in a remote village, Geyre. He noticed that the old men in the village coffee shop were sitting on top of ruins, which he later discovered belonged to the ancient city of Aphrodisias.[II]

II   Ara Güler, *Aphrodisias* (Istanbul: Ara Güler Archives and Research Center, 2019), p. 53.

WHY DEMOLISH?

Architectures are the places where the stories happen. Sometimes exterior influences put an end to the stories and narratives prematurely, but leave the architectures behind. The architectures then serve to house new stories.[17] — KARIN REISINGER

Beauty is not created solely by the artist, it is completed by the citizens, the users, and the spectators, who by so doing contribute to its creation.[18] — KISHŌ KUROKAWA

For some, demolishing is a euphorically victorious act, a kind of choreography where the dancers – the dust heaps and rubble – gradually vanish.

Demolishing is a spectacular performance. Though it is an act of violence, it is considered an innocent option in urban discussions, as if the city will be able to take a deep breath from the void achieved by demolition. The urban void becomes a canvas onto which people can project their fantasies and desires.

Unlucky Stars

There are times when the planet needs to make fundamental changes that result in the reformation of the existing landscape. As humans, we call them natural disasters, but in fact they are just 'unlucky

17 Karin Reisinger, 'Abandoned architectures: Some dirty narratives,' in *Architecture and Feminisms: Ecologies, Economies, Technologies*, ed. Hélène Frichot, Catharina Gabrielsson and Helen Runting (London: Routledge, 2017), p. 207.

18 Kishō Kurokawa, *Metabolism in Architecture* (London: Studio Vista, 1977), p. 33.

stars', as in the Latin root of the word 'disaster'. What makes these natural events disasters is that the necessities of human-made environments do not overlap with geological activities; natural events tend to decrease the order established by humans and other living things. Earthquakes are among the disasters that reshape the existing environment, both human-made and natural.

On 6 February 2023, two devastating earthquakes hit Kahramanmaraş, a city in the south-eastern part of Turkey. The city centre was heavily damaged, with many buildings destroyed. Just a couple of months before the earthquakes, Kahramanmaraş Special Provincial Administration renowned as 'The Ugliest Building in the World' – an eighteen-storey public building at the heart of Kahramanmaraş that had been abandoned for a couple of years – was demolished. It took almost six months to completely demolish the structurally robust building, which would have remained safe in an earthquake. In order to justify demolishing the 'ugly' structure – called the Yellow Building by locals – the municipality designated a forty-hectare zone as an urban regeneration area, based on the earthquake risk of the city centre. The plan was either to repair or demolish the risky buildings. However, the only buildings in the urban regeneration area that were completely demolished by the municipality before the earthquake were the Yellow Building and the adjacent court house. After the earthquake, the majority of the buildings that surrounded it fell or were heavily damaged. Instead of spending the energy and funding on making buildings earthquake resilient, the priority of the municipality was to get rid of the harmless 'ugly' building.

As much as being an object of collective disgust, the Yellow Building was also loved. Young locals described it as 'the only non-boring thing on the high street', meeting and gathering around it.[19]

A colourful giant cake stands on the pavement, commemorating the building, which now lacks its tricolored façade cladding and will soon to be completely demolished. People are taking selfies with the cake, with the outworn building in the background as a farewell to the giant structure.

Although surveys indicate that almost 50% of the locals want the building to remain,[20] there are still locals who support the demolition for various reasons. Some argue that its height ruins the city's silhouette. Others

19   Emine Nur Uzdil, interviewed by the author, 30 March 2023.

20   Arif Şentek, 'Sarı Binanın Serüveni' [The Journey of the Yellow Building], *Bianet – Bağımsız İletişim Ağı*, 2 October 2021, bianet.org/biamag/kultur/251165-sari-binanin-seruveni.

view its postmodern architecture as problematic and believe it should be removed. However, as Reinier de Graaf has pointed out, buildings have no alternative but to function based on the principles of capital. Therefore, the true distinction is perhaps not between modern or postmodern architecture, but rather 'architecture before and after its annexation by capital'.[21] The Yellow Building was demolished because it no longer provided the image of a profitable asset. Just as a scriptwriter might need to kill off a protagonist in order to take a story in a new direction, the Yellow Building had to be demolished in order to pave the way for a new narrative of capitalisation.

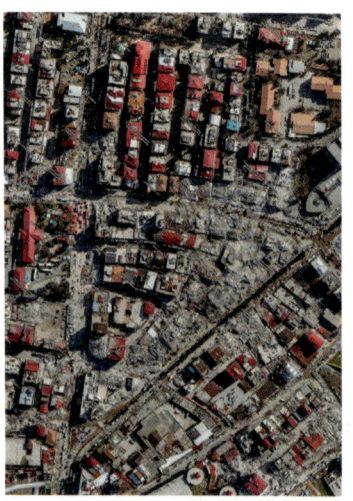

Requests to purchase and repurpose the property were rejected because the primary motive behind the demolition of the building was to capitalise on the land it occupied. This was to be achieved through the establishment of a new mixed-use building complex that involved a different set of stakeholders in a new embodiment.

Aerial view of the site of the Yellow Building and its surroundings, Kahramanmaraş

21   Reinier de Graaf, 'Architecture Is Now a Tool of Capital, Complicit in a Purpose Antithetical to its Social Mission', *Architectural Review*, 21 July 2020, architectural-review.com/essays/architecture-is-now-a-tool-of-capital-complicit-in-a-purpose-antithetical-to-its-social-mission.

After the demolition of the façade, its architect, Arif Nafiz Aköz pointed out that even though the building would look a little more slender when the cladding was removed, there was still no way that such an imposing building could say 'I do not exist'[22]

Dismantling of Nakagin Capsule Tower

In the same year that the Yellow Building was demolished, another tower was dismantled in a different part of the world. This region is also known for experiencing earthquakes, and the tower had previously survived many of them. However, despite its resilience, it was eventually taken apart. The

22 'Bir Yıkımın Öyküsü: Kahramanmaraş İl Özel İdare Binası' [Story of a Destruction: Kahramanmaraş Special Provincial Administration], *Serbest Mimar*, no. 46 (December 2022): 22–27.

Nakagin Capsule Tower was a tall, modular building in the centre of Tokyo, designed by Kishō Kurokawa. But instead of standing out like the Yellow Building, it was hidden among other structures in the dense city. Made up of small capsules stacked on top of each other, it was initially designed to 'herald the era of moving architecture'.[23] However, the capsules never moved after they were assembled on the tower structure, though anchored with only four bolts. The reason why is the same as the reason why they could never be renovated: in order to detach one capsule, all 140 had to be removed because the gap between them was only 30 cm, making it impossible to reach the joints without disassembling them all.[24]

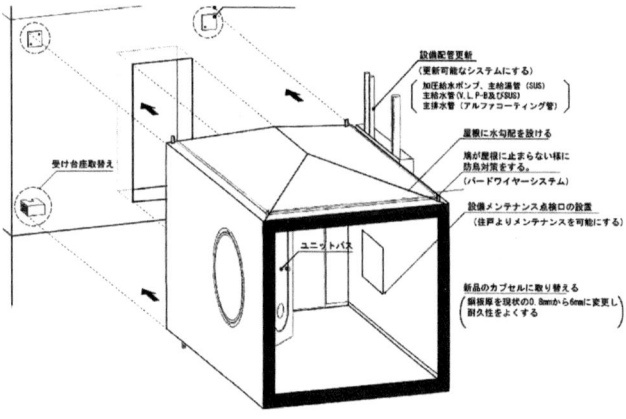

設備配管更新
（更新可能なシステムにする）
加圧給水ポンプ、主枝湯管（SUS）
主枝水管（V、L F-B及びSUS）
主排水管（アルファコーティング管）

屋根に水勾配を設ける

鳩が屋根に止まらない様に
防鳥対策をする。
（バードワイヤーシステム）

設備メンテナンス点検口の設置
（住戸よりメンテナンスを可能にする）

受け台座取替え

ユニットバス

新品のカプセルに取り替える
（鋼板厚を現状の0.8mmから6mmに変更し）
耐久性をよくする

In 2006, Kurokawa redesigned the capsules, but the renovation project was never realised. [III]

23 'Capsule Declaration, Article 2', *SD Magazine*, 1969.

24 Tatsuyuki Maeda and Yuka Yoshida, 'The Real Reason Why Nakagin Capsule Tower Was Never Metabolized', *Docomomo Journal*, 1 January 2021, doi.org/10.52200/65.a.voj1oe9b, p. 118.

III Zhongjie Lin, 'Nakagin Capsule Tower Revisiting the Future of the Recent Past', *Journal of Architectural Education* (1984–) 65, no. 1 (2011): 13–32.

Nakagin Capsule Tower, which was built in 1972 and demolished in 2022, was the symbol of Metabolist architecture, which in Kurokawa's words, aims to 'grow and change perfectly'. For Kurokawa, Metabolist architecture has to be beautiful and able to 'discover a new aesthetic based on movement'.[25] Unlike the Yellow Building, which gained popularity due to its 'ugliness', the Capsule Tower was initially renowned for its beauty, particularly among modernism enthusiasts. Yet, despite the fight for its renovation by Kurokawa, residents of Capsule Tower voted for its demolition.[26] A considerable number found it ugly and disturbing. In an interview, Kurokawa explained that the majority of residents inherited the capsules from the preceding generation, who, unlike their children, may have enjoyed living in them.[27]

Undoubtedly, aesthetic discussions are just the visible and easily comprehensible part of the 'negotiated order' that surrounds buildings.[28] The act of demolition is not merely physical destruction, but also involves the disassembling of existing power structures, economic systems, and the uncanny tales of ghosts. The removal of the ghost itself is necessary in order to generate a Hero as a fresh figure on the stage.

25 Rem Koolhaas, Hans Ulrich Obrist, Kayoko Ota and James Westcott, *Project Japan: Metabolism Talks* (Cologne: Taschen, 2011).

26 Ibid.

27 Ashley Rawlings, 'Political Architecture: Interview with Kishō Kurokawa', *Tokyo Art Beat*, 5 February 2011, tokyoartbeat.com/en/articles/-/political-architecture-interview-with-kisho-kurokawa.

28 Stephen M. Graham and Nigel Thrift, 'Out of Order', *Theory, Culture & Society* 24, no. 3 (1 May 2007): 4.

Lego model of Nakagin Capsule Tower

CSI

Our work … is about developing and augmenting the capacity to notice, to register those traces … Then we need to connect them – one trace to the other. In that sense, our work is like a detective. We look at the past in order to transform the future.[29] — EYAL WEIZMAN

Demolishing a building creates a *tabula rasa* on which a techno-heroic story can be written more rapidly. The Latin phrase *tabula rasa* is usually interpreted as 'clean slate', but it literally means 'scraped tablet'. If scraping refers to erasing the existing, then we need to accept that a *tabula rasa* can never be a clean slate. It requires

29   Rebecca Ildikó Leete, 'Eyal Weizman on Forensic Architecture: "Mapping Is Power"', *ArchDaily*, 3 June 2022, archdaily.com/982954/eyal-weizman-on-forensic-architecture-mapping-is-power.

the existing structures to be rubbed out, dug up and remade. Just as an eraser cannot completely remove every trace from paper, a *tabula rasa* is never completely empty. Even when cleaned, the traces remain. Though we have treated the *tabula rasa* as a blank white page, it holds information, much like a crime scene, where every detail needs to be investigated and carefully scrutinised. This is what intimidates architects, contractors, landlords and anyone who is involved in the process of construction. Before technology was developed to clean the slate, to make it look brand new, and to annihilate what already exists on it, the site was a carrier bag containing information about the Earth and the society.

On Halloween 2022, Boston Dynamics posted a video on Instagram. It starts with clichés of Halloween, such as spider webs, black bats and dark ghostly images. As the spooky music continues, a bright yellow robot dog enters the scene, walking in between the corridors of a decrepit building: Spot for Ghost Hunting.

Spot in operation

The agile robot created by Boston Dynamics confidently moves through abandoned buildings to make surveys and analysis in areas that human beings cannot access for health and safety reasons. Spot functions almost like a forensic architect/engineer, investigating the causes of damage and deterioration and recording any evidence found inside the building.

If technology is used more efficiently for investigating and diagnosing existing structures, then these structures become compelling rather than being intimidating.

CONCRESCERE / GROW TOGETHER

The world would be a safer place if concrete was translucent. This is the problem: it's too easy to cheat.[30] — ROSS STEIN

There is also a kind of powder which from natural causes produces astonishing results. It is found in the neighbourhood of Baiae and in the country belonging to the towns round about Mt Vesuvius. This substance, when mixed with lime and rubble, not only lends strength to buildings of other kinds, but even when piers of it are constructed in the sea, they set hard under water. The reason for this seems to be that the soil on the slopes of the mountains in these neighbourhoods is hot and full of hot springs. This would not be so unless the mountains had beneath them huge fires of burning sulphur or alum or asphalt. So the fire and the heat of the flames, coming up hot from far within through the fissures, make the soil there light, and the tufa found there is spongy and free

30   Interview with Ross Stein by Andrea Thompson, 'Why the Earthquake in Turkey Was So Damaging and Deadly', *Scientific American*, 6 February 2023, scientificamerican.com/article/why-the-earthquake-in-turkey-was-so-damaging-and-deadly.

from moisture. Hence, when the three substances, all formed on a similar principle by the force of fire, are mixed together, the water suddenly taken in makes them cohere, and the moisture quickly hardens them so that they set into a mass which neither the waves nor the force of the water can dissolve.[31] — VITRUVIUS, 'Pozzolana'

When Vitruvius described the formula of Pozzolana – the significant element of Roman Concrete – with mountains, hot springs, fire and water, it was as if he were describing a baking recipe using ingredients from nature. Yet the modern recipe for concrete would include exploded mines, cacophonous factories, giant mixers. As with many building materials, the history of concrete is the history of the human-nature relationship. As the distance between the two grows and the relationship becomes more complex, the content, the methods

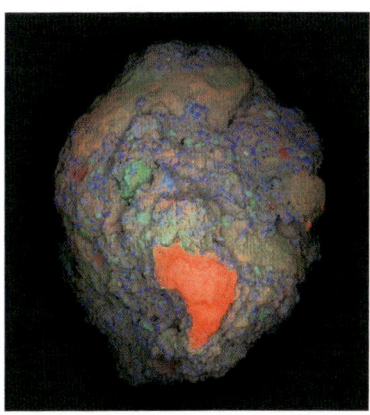

A recent study by a team of researchers led by Admir Masic[IV] reveals the formula of the concrete used in the enduring structures of Ancient Rome. The formula includes calcium-rich lime clast – the part in red shown here – which makes Roman concrete self-healing.

31   Vitruvius, *The Ten Books on Architecture: Elibron Classics* (Cambridge: Harvard University Press, 1914), p. 46.

IV   Linda M. Seymour et al, 'Hot mixing: Mechanistic insights into the durability of ancient Roman concrete', *Science Advances*, 9 (1), 2023.

of production, and finally the end product evolve. This evolution of rapid production and accessible ingredients makes concrete the most widely used material in the world. Yet modern concrete is not as durable as its ancestor, which is still appreciated in examples of historical building that have defied time for centuries. Concrete is often blamed for a range of major problems facing humanity today, such as the climate crisis, groundwater depletion, uncontrolled urban sprawl and building collapses during earthquakes. With its easy-to-pour-difficult-to-change structure, concrete is charged with every crime, even when it may not be directly responsible.

The process of constructing and demolishing with concrete involves a spectacle of dust and rubble that begins with dynamiting mines to extract concrete ingredients, and ends with dynamiting concrete buildings to be demolished. This cloud of debris and dust is the inevitable outcome of using concrete as a construction material, from the initial stages of obtaining raw materials to the final stages of demolition.

For spectacle lovers, if there is no chance to bring the Hero back to his glory days, demolition seems to be the best option. If a reason is needed to justify the act, the best option is the neglected condition of the Hero, which is most of the time made of concrete. Modern concrete, if not cared for properly, becomes weak and brittle.

The word 'concrete' comes from the Latin term *concrescere*, which means to grow together. The original recipe for concrete by the Romans was specifically developed to 'grow together' rather than to expire in time. Yet concrete now is the most inflexible ingredient of existing buildings. The ancient formula included

seawater,[32] as well as volcanic ash, once filling up
the porous structure of concrete to prevent bacteria,
which has been an enemy of contemporary concrete
since the original recipe changed. If technology
had been used to develop healing methods for
concrete, as much as it had been for reconstruction
methods, buildings would not expire so fast.

**Ancient recipes for concrete reveal that concrete was reinforced
with the help of nature, protecting it from slowly decaying from
outdoor conditions. Using technology mimicking nature, bacteria
that heal concrete are currently being developed by researchers.[V]**

Türkiye came first on the list of cement exporting
countries until 2013.[33] In 2021, the Top 250
Contractors in the World list included forty Turkish
companies, with Türkiye coming third after China

32 'How Seawater Strengthens Ancient Roman Concrete', *Unews*, 3 July 2017,
unews.utah.edu/roman-concrete.

33 Bora Çevik, 'Çimento Sektörü', 2016, ekonomi.isbank.com.tr/
ContentManagement/Documents/sr201604_cimentosektoru.pdf.

V   'Using bacteria to make self-healing concrete', *Microbiology Society*,
youtube.com/watch?v=H7frDSx9js8.

and the US.[34] How is it possible that this success story ended with the death of more than 50,000 in earthquakes in the southeast of Türkiye on February 2023, mostly due to the poor quality and condition of concrete structures? In fact, the reason underlying this contradictory outcome is the same reason why there are hundreds of abandoned buildings dispersed around the country: the main goal of construction is not to achieve safe and sound buildings, but to build as quickly and profitably as possible. In this sense, the devastating ruins left in the wake of earthquakes, composed mainly of concrete rubble, is not directly related to concrete itself, but rather to the collapsed economic and political mechanisms that surround concrete production and the construction industry.

Concrete sample from Kahramanmaraş from the rubble after the earthquakes. The aggregates in the sample are much bigger than they are supposed to be, measuring almost 8-9 cm.

34   'World's Top 250 International Contractors Announced: There are 40 Turkish Companies on the List', *T24*, 25 August 2021, t24.com.tr/haber/ dunyanin-en-buyuk-250-uluslararasi-muteahhidi-aciklandi-listede-40-turk-sirket-var,974391.

REPAIR SHOP

We need a generation of architects who do not indulge in the madness of building but take part in repair.[35] — MARINA TABASSUM

Given the degree of brokenness of the broken world (and the expense of fixing it), we need *all* maintainers to apply their diverse disciplinary methods and practical skills to the collective project of repair.[36] — SHANNON MATTERN

Without even requiring technological advancements, buildings can last for many years if they are properly maintained. Machines are repaired to be stronger and more sound, but when it comes to buildings, repair primarily aims for a better look, rather than a stronger structure. Yet repairing a building is not just a matter of decoration; it involves design considerations such as the structure, space, façade and even the building's relationship with the surrounding city.

But how can repair challenge reconstruction if the whole construction industry and its side branches are incentivised for reconstructing rather than repairing? Why would architects choose to repair if the primary motive of their education and the main expectation from their practice requires an object that is designed from scratch?

35 Marina Tabassum, 'Letter to a Young Architect', Architectural Review, 22 September 2020, architectural-review.com/essays/letters-to-a-young-architect/marina-tabassum-letter-to-a-young-architect.

36 Shannon Mattern, 'Maintenance and Care', *Places Journal*, November 2018, doi.org/10.22269/181120.

The world constantly needs repair, even though we tend to neglect the networks of repair in daily life. In a country where three quarters of its cities are in earthquake zones, we have to repair a huge building stock to prepare for these events. We must redefine repair as a practice where design, craft and engineering all come together.

Six-storey building in Istanbul reinforced with steel

VENICE CHARTER – REVISITED

It is a simple tale: Taxidermy was made into the servant of the 'real'.[37] — DONNA HARAWAY

...'protection' in heritage contexts applies not just to the physical form of discrete objects and structures but to those who own them and those who encounter them.[38] — CAITLIN DESILVEY

In 1964, a group of conservation professionals in Venice prepared the Venice Charter[39] for the Conservation and Restoration of Monuments and Sites. In Article 9 of the sixteen-article charter, the aim of restoring old buildings was defined as 'to preserve and reveal the aesthetic and historical value of the monument ... based on respect for original material and authentic documents. It must stop at the point where conjecture begins'.

A taxidermist building the structure of a bull-giraffe to be displayed in the American Museum of Natural History in 1927

37   Donna Haraway, 'Teddy Bear Patriarchy: Taxidermy in the Garden of Eden, New York City, 1908–1936', *Social Text*, No. 11 (Winter, 1984–1985): 20–64.

38   DeSilvey, op. cit. p. 15.

39   International Charter for the Conversation and Restoration of Monuments and Sites (The Venice Charter, 1964), *Scientific Journal*, ICOMOS – International Council on Monuments and Sites, 1994, icomos.org/images/DOCUMENTS/Charters/Venice_Charter_EN_2023.pdf.

Current debates on preservation question the concepts, methods and the aims of preserving. As Parreno suggests, inspired by Haraway, rather than a 'taxidermic preservation' that sees today as an extension of the past, preservation can instead become an operation for creating a better future, bridging the gap between what has happened and what could happen.[40] What if preservation leads us to conjecture rather than certainty?

Preservation is the opposite of transformation. The main desire underlying the act of preservation is to take the Hero back to his glory days, to respect the original and authentic and never add anything to it. It aims to conserve aesthetics and historical value at all costs. But today, as Shannon Mattern reminds us, preserving our human world may sometimes conflict with taking care of the planet.[41]

When the time period between the present and what is preserved narrows down, preservation becomes an activity about what we are currently building. Rem Koolhaas points out that preservation is no longer an activity about the past, but a way to look at the future.[42] Is the term 'preservation' itself undergoing a transformation?*

40   Christian Parreno. 'Architectural Preservation as Taxidermy: Patriarchy and Boredom.' In *Architecture and Feminisms Ecologies, Economies, Technologies*, edited by Hélène Frichot, Catharina Gabrielsson, and Helen Runting. (New York: Routledge, 2018).

41   Mattern, op. cit.

42   Rem Koolhaas, *Preservation is Overtaking Us* (New York: GSAPP Books, 2014).

*   Please see p. 100 for 'Venice Charter – Revisited'.

LEARNING FROM

Denise Scott Brown, – shown in Las Vegas in the photo – points out how *The Carrier Bag Theory of Architecture* fits with her own understanding of urban planning and design as she's always spoken of her 'bag of tools' for architects which also influenced her revolutionary view of Las Vegas.[VI]

Though discussions of architecture mainly revolve around either objects or architects, it is relationships that make architecture possible. Simple or complicated, depending on the theme, relationships embody the immaterial structure of architecture. However, they require a concentrated focus and elaborate scrutiny to be discovered, since they are not the visible, apparent face of architecture.
We need to learn from relationships. When Denise Scott Brown, Robert Venturi and their team of students and architect researchers visited Las Vegas in 1968, their aim was to learn from the existing landscape. They wrote, 'learning from the existing landscape is a

VI   Denise Scott Brown, e-mail to author, 12 April 2023.

way of being revolutionary for an architect'.[43] In the 1960s being revolutionary in architecture generally referred to the modern movement, but they were clearly not referring to that kind of revolution, 'which is to tear down Paris and begin again, as Le Corbusier suggested in the 1920s, but another, more tolerant way; that is, to question how we look at things'.[44]

There are certain reasons why Scott Brown, Venturi and their team call this action 'learning from the existing landscape' rather than reading, analysing or rethinking the existing. These verbs position the existing entity as a passive subject, whereas 'learning from' suggests a more active and engaged approach. Learning from the existing is not a pre-study for design, it is the design itself. It is a proactive strategy that also considers its subject – either a town or a building – as something with which to be in dialogue. When Scott Brown and Venturi found the ugly and the ordinary more interesting than the heroic and original, this approach was revolutionary in the academic world.

In fact, even today, our curricula need to fundamentally change to include a 'learning from' philosophy. We inevitably focus on the teachable while we prepare curricula. We first show students how to clean their minds from the previous images and narratives they have inherited, and then they create Pinterest boards full of images representing the new legacy we teach them. What if we were to include more courses on how to transform existing structures in

43 Robert Venturi, Denise Scott Brown and Steven Izenour, *Learning from Las Vegas* (Cambridge, MA: MIT Press, 2017).

44 Ibid.

our curriculum? Structures of power, technology, the history of both the human and non-human, as well as relations of objects, buildings and materials are to be excavated first and then transformed based on needs.

Undoubtedly, it takes more energy and more inter-disciplinary work to learn from and teach a messy, entangled curriculum that involves the unlearning of our previous knowledge of the past, present and future. As Shannon Mattern suggested, 'to study maintenance is itself an act of maintenance'.[45] Similarly, we could argue that studying transformation is, in itself, a transformative act.

But would this fundamental change help to get rid of the Hero in stories in which we ourselves have been part of the invasion? Revolutionising the academy is challenging because it demands not only a change in the content but also a simultaneous change in ourselves.

If decision-makers and the construction industry, along with technology providers and architecture schools, prioritise existing structures as a primary focus rather than a specialised area, we will all have the opportunity to learn from the intricacy and variety of chaos and disorder.

> This 'safe space' is to be created, protected by universities so the next generation can ask better questions – universities are just looking for better answers.[46] — LESLEY LOKKO

45 Mattern, op. cit.

46 'Francesca Hughes and Lesley Lokko on a Future for Architectural Education', *Architectural Review*, 12 November 2021, architectural-review. com/essays/pedagogy/francesca-hughes-and-lesley-lokko-on-a-future-for-architectural-education.

TEST DRIVE

let me sing you the blues
not of pretty but of truths[47] — TURGUT UYAR

Technology and science have primarily been developed
to provide a cleared and flattened land for construction
purposes, as well as to introduce advanced techniques
that enable new Heroes to emerge. But if 'technology
and science are refined as primarily cultural carrier
bags rather than a weapon of domination',[48] as Le Guin
proposed, architecture would have a broader range of
tools at its disposal for transforming existing structures.

When working with an existing structure, the main
challenge is to envision its future stages. How will the
first occupants enliven these abandoned structures? If
technology equips us with the tools to dream alternative
futures without preconceptions or predetermined
paths, then we can see our vast collection of existing
buildings as carrier bags, as containers of stories,
and more importantly, as future resources.

There are numerous abandoned buildings scattered
around the world that currently have no occupants
to revive them. It is the people who keep buildings
alive, and it is the buildings that keep people together.
Architecture starts this symbiotic relationship.
Architecture enlivens. Yet our perceptions of beauty,
functionality and other preconceived notions can
influence our thinking and block our ability to imagine
beyond the inherited images to which we have been

47 Turgut Uyar, *Büyük Saat* [The Big Watch] (Istanbul: YKY, 2022).
48 Le Guin, op. cit.

exposed. Although it may take time to reject our preconceptions and challenge our inherited ways of thinking, technology can help us envision potential changes, overcome our mental barriers and make a test drive for the second life of a structure.

If we train an AI model using hundreds of datasets of unused buildings, we can envision potential ways to enliven these empty structures. This process can provide a demonstration of a possible future – not a techno-heroic one, but a realistic one.

Colomina and Wigley noted that the scale figures in architects' sketches are 'the protohumans that test-drive the prototypes of modern design'.[VII] Here, AI figures take the place of the scale figures, and test-drive the reanimation of abandoned buildings.

VII   Beatriz Colomina and Mark Wigley, *Are We Human?: Notes on an Archaeology of Design* (Baden: Lars Müller Publishers, 2016).

TRANSFORMERS

Always transform, with and for the inhabitants.[49]

— LACATON & VASSAL

Although transforming existing structures was the primary method of construction for early humans, it has become a niche practice in contemporary architecture over the centuries. During their Pritzker award speech in 2001, Herzog & de Meuron, whose highest-profile project at the time was an adaptive reuse of a former power station as a museum, Tate Modern, explained their strategy for transforming the existing structures as 'a kind of Aikido strategy, where you use your enemy's energy for your own purposes.'[50] The enemy here was the existing building. The architect was battling the enemy, but not with a weapon.

Just a couple of years after their statement about how to transform buildings, they started work on the project of Elbphilarmonie, which was a former warehouse to be transformed into an events hall. Here, their Aikido strategy almost turned into a disaster – as the duo called it. It was a mega-project, finished seven years later and more than ten times over budget. 'We thought

49   Barbara Miglietti, 'Never Demolish. Always Transform, with and for the Inhabitants': Anne Lacaton Delivers Inaugural Jaqueline Tyrwhitt Urban Design Lecture', Harvard Graduate School of Design, 14 April 2022, gsd. harvard.edu/2022/04/never-demolish-always-transform-with-and-for-the-inhabitants-anne-lacaton-on-urban-design-and-architecture.

50   Pritzker Prize, 'Jacques Herzog and Pierre de Meuron, 2001 Laureates Biography', 2001, pritzkerprize.com/sites/default/files/inline-files/2001_bio.pdf.

it was going to destroy us,'[51] said Herzog & de Meuron, when the project finally opened its doors to the public. The energy of the enemy – the former warehouse – was much greater than the architects had initially estimated.

The final appearance of Elbphilarmonie in Hamburg, opened in 2016, resembles a frozen Aikido scene.

When the Elbphilharmonie project was completed, the architects involved in it were so utterly exhausted that they became convinced that architecture could no longer be done in the same way as they had been doing it before. They said that they may be the last generation of 'author' style architects who will get the chance to build a colossal project.[52]

51   Oliver Wainwright, 'We Thought It Was Going to Destroy Us ... Herzog and De Meuron's Hamburg Miracle', *The Guardian*, 4 November 2016, theguardian. com/artanddesign/2016/nov/04/hamburg-elbphilhamonie-herzog-de-meuron-a-cathedral-for-our-time.

52   Ibid.

Before (left) and after (right)
Transformation of 530 Dwellings - Grand Parc Bordeaux

When Lacaton & Vassal won the Pritzker award
two decades later, Anne Lacaton said that they see
'everything existing in the project as an opportunity'
and they 'take care ... of the existing, not in the way
of protection or too much respect but as a resource.'[53]
Rather than seeking the chance to build extravagant
projects, Lacaton & Vassal gave a chance to existing
buildings by transforming them and giving them a
second life. Lacaton's definition of transformation
was a sobering one: 'It isn't a question of "one or the
other" but a question of "one and the other".'[54]

53 Louisiana Channel, 'Anne Lacaton Interview: Always Add', 21 August 2018,
youtube.com/watch?v=evqj_lCSjKo.

54 Muck Petzet and Florian Heilmeyer, *Reduce, Reuse, Recycle: Architecture
as Resource*, German Pavilion, 13th International Architecture Exhibition,
Venice Biennale 2012.

Neither battle nor too much respect: unheroic, but fresh.

Unlike the Elbphilarmonie, the exterior photos of the Transformation of 530 Dwellings project by Lacaton & Vassal with Druot and Hutin reveal little about the building's use. It is impossible to fully appreciate their architecture by merely standing in front of the building, since the glass façade appears to be just another example of contemporary building design. To fully comprehend the transformative effect of their architecture, one needs to physically enter the building and experience the space directly.

THE POOL

When Ursula K. Le Guin explained *The Carrier Bag Theory of Fiction*, she claimed that 'the men and women in the wild-oat patch and their kids and the skills of makers and the thoughts of the thoughtful and the songs of the singers are all part of'[55] the scene where the Hero seems to be battling the enemy alone. Yet, they were not part of the story. The way in which the origins of culture are explained has an impact not only on evolution and fiction but also on architecture. The history of architecture has traditionally focused on highlighting the architect as an individual figure, just as the narrative of human history has tended to centre around a solitary Hero rather than a collaborative effort.

55   Le Guin, op. cit.

When Beatriz Colomina revealed the secret of modern architecture as collaboration,[56] she pointed out that the concept of the individual author and the building as an art object have received more attention and acceptance from historians, journalists and institutions compared to the collaborative and messy nature of the architectural practice.[57] For a long while, it was his story, not theirs. This depiction resembles the scene of daily life that Le Guin described: the lone hero battling mammoths while everyone else in the scene was 'pressed into the service in the tale of the Hero'.[58] Both Colomina and Le Guin were interested in exploring what happens beyond the lens of the camera, which often overlooks the other figures and actions that are essential for sustaining life.

If we define architecture as a collaborative and messy process, then transforming an existing building lies at the heart of it, rather than being a secondary consideration. Landlords, contractors, investors and architects may be wary of working with an existing building, since every stone that is touched has the potential to bring unforeseen trouble and complications. Existing buildings are complex and unpredictable. When navigating complex and unpredictable situations, architecture can be an even messier and more challenging practice.

56   Beatriz Colomina, 'Outrage: Blindness to Women Turns out to Be Blindness to Architecture Itself', *Architectural Review*, 8 March 2018, architectural-review.com/essays/outrage/outrage-blindness-to-women-turns-out-to-be-blindness-to-architecture-itself.

57   Ibid.

58   Le Guin, op. cit.

But in fact, architecture can become a tool to handle unpredictability as well as complexity and diversity. In this age of economic, political and ecological crisis, architecture, like every other profession, requires a fundamental shift. Instead of a narrative of battles, of heroic styles, of fighting with the forces, of large budgets, we need a new theory of the ordinary, of learning from, of transformations, and of handling unpredictability. Then, finally, Le Guin's dream may come true. The image that deserves to be engraved on the walls of a cave is of those who gather oats and carry them in their bags rather than those who hunt mammoths with their spears.

Can we, as architects, accept such a profound transformation in the established images we have inherited and our rigid ideas of what constitutes beauty and functionality? Are we ready to merge our designs with existing structures instead of simply replacing them?

What if we no longer have to carve, dig, excavate or extract to start a building, but instead to listen and accompany, to fill and merge, to speak and learn from it? What if the building is the carrier bag for new structures and stories?

Similar to a movie that ends with a wedding scene, when the real journey is only just beginning, the story of architecture often ends when construction is completed and before people begin to inhabit the space. It is not a coincidence that most photos of buildings illustrating their architectural features are without humans. Undoubtedly, there has been considerable research on the after-life of buildings in the last decades. Yet it is newly completed buildings and their stories that mainly occupy mainstream design media. Whether human or non-human, any subject in a scene that is not part of the design can distract the viewer. However, that is life. Life begins in the buildings we design after we have left the stage and people arrive to inhabit them.

Finally, it will take time to learn to weave or to fabricate (in the word 'architect', 'tect' comes from the same root as the term for 'weave') a genuine relationship with existing structures. 'Learning, then, is all about evolution, mutations of the gene pool that transform but never fully depart from the past and the present',[59] says Colomina.

Our theory was born with a pool – an abandoned swimming pool where only seagulls enjoyed the water. This is where our conversation with ghosts started. These conversations not only inspired the transformation of the pool but also led us to construct a new architectural theory. The pool makes us withdraw ourselves from the heroic story, trying to transform the inherited images in our minds, just like the ones engraved in the caves.

The pool paves the way for this urgent question, to which *The Carrier Bag Theory of Architecture* might respond: why should we keep a building that is not functional and beautiful? The response arose when substituting 'functional and beautiful' with 'meaningful and resourceful'. Any building can become meaningful

59   Beatriz Colomina, 'Five Voices: On Denise Scott Brown', *Soane*, 2018, soane.org/soane-medal/2018-denise-scott-brown/five-voices-denise-scott-brown.

and resourceful if we engage in conversation with it to unlearn our preconceived assumptions. Instead of demolishing it, we kept the pool because its structure provided us with an empty container when we drained it. We kept the blue tiles as the remnants of the past style, not because of our respect for the style itself, but in order to present the information that this place was once a swimming pool. This reveals the political history that the campus had been privately used by the previous mayors, despite being public property. The new design would mediate this story to the next generations.

Similar to a swimming pool, which looks compelling only when it is filled with water, the public pool needs people to emphasise the idea of transformation. The container to let the water flow now serves for the people to flow.

This is how *The Carrier Bag Theory of Architecture* was derived from the transformation of an abandoned swimming pool into a public pool of listening and sharing.

Before the building that represents power, there was the building that includes people.

**The pool at Istanbul Planning Agency (IPA) Campus
after transformation in 2022**

Public event at the pool on the IPA Campus

A Manifesto for
The Carrier Bag Theory of Architecture

☺ Story

Building as a container, as a carrier bag, as a pool that holds the life story of transformations, unpredictability and messiness. If we define the building as a container, then the building becomes the site itself and architecture no longer needs empty plots to flourish, but existing structures to begin the transformation.

⌣¹ Theory

The Carrier Bag Theory of Fiction by Ursula K. Le Guin questions the stories and heroes we have been told and the images we have inherited. Can we change our ossified perceptions of beauty and functionality? The answer is yes, when we define architecture with stories rather than objects.

In 2021, the world's oldest woven basket was found in Muraba'at Cave, preserved for 10,500 years thanks to the dry climate.

⌣2⌣ **Addiction**

Construction becomes an addiction when triggered by economic reasons rather than spatial needs.

Ankapark, Ankara, 2023

Ankapark, Ankara, 2023

⌣3⌣ **Ghosts**

The Carrier Bag Theory of Architecture begins with revealing the story of the neglected. Though their absence is unnoticed, they change the whole scenography once they are uncovered and pulled on stage. What if we listen to and understand the stories of abandoned buildings, rather than focusing on more heroic, successful examples?

Apartment Building in Kasımpaşa, Istanbul

Çukobirlik General Directorate, Adana

Metropol, Mersin. Architect: Cengiz Bektaş

Anatolian (Public) High School, Samsun

İTÜ Eko Yapı Research Centre, Istanbul

Caprice Gold Hotel, Istanbul

Ziraat Bank Recreational Facility, Aydın

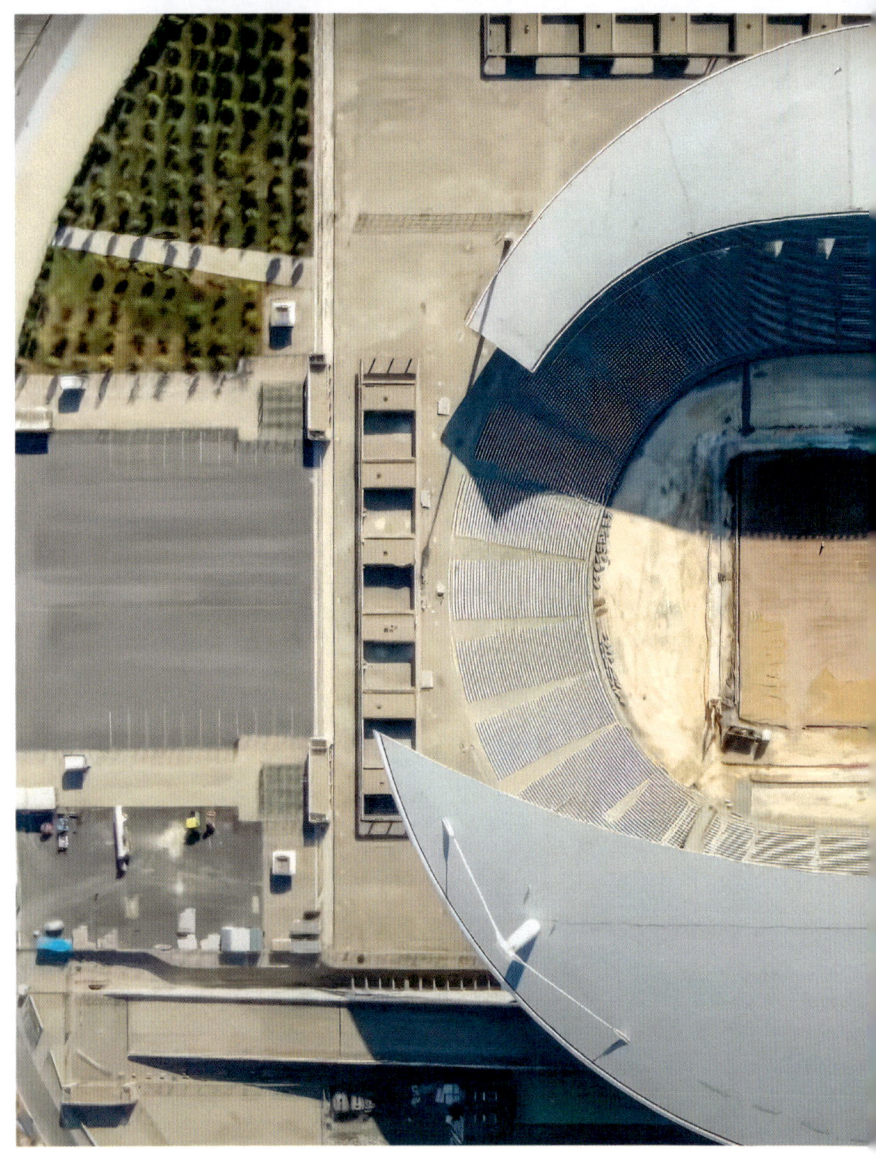

Olympic Stadium, Istanbul

‿4‿ **Entropy**

Abandoned buildings are entropic. They are the extensions of a rearranged landscape with their chaotic structures open to possibilities. They are the abundant resource of materials and memory that could restrain humans from constantly reshaping earth.

Atakent Anatolian (Public) High School, İzmir

Petrol Station, Bursa

Hilton Hotel, İzmir

Alsancak Silos, İzmir

Lodging, Zonguldak

Sümerbank Print Factory, Nazilli, Aydın

⌣5⌣ **Expiry Date**

Heroes have expiry dates, buildings don't. Making a building is the result of a compromise and when the compromise is no longer available, buildings expire.

⎝6⎠ **Why Demolish?**

We demolish because we cannot tolerate the ugly, the old, the outdated and the unused. As resources diminish, we can no longer afford this highly choreographed performance that hurts the Earth. It has become necessary to listen to and work with buildings' stories rather than placing them on pedestals or discarding and erasing them completely.

⑦ CSI

In a time when a whole building can be scanned, even by a smartphone, can we use technology to investigate and diagnose existing buildings more efficiently? Can technology save buildings from being fragile heroes?

⌣8⌣ **Concrescere***

The original recipe of concrete was specifically developed by the Romans to 'grow together' rather than to expire with time as in the case of the contemporary formula of concrete.
We need to reconsider our relationship with concrete which constitutes the majority of existing buildings.

* The root of the word concrete in Latin, *concrescere*, means growing together.

A destroyed building in southeast Turkey damaged by the earthquakes in 2023

⑨ Repair Shop

Machines are repaired to be stronger and more sound. Buildings too, regularly need to be repaired, not with a superficial make-over, but with in-depth care, carried out collaboratively through engineering, craft and design.

(10) Venice Charter – Revisited

The opposite of transformation is preservation. Preservation desires to take the Hero back to his glory days, whereas transformation does not need a Hero, it just needs a story to cultivate.

Venice Charter – Revisited

for the sake of the Ghosts

DEFINITIONS

Article 1.
The concept of ~~a historic monument~~ **existing structures** embraces not only the single architectural work but also the urban or rural setting in which is found the evidence of a particular ~~civilization~~ **organisation**, a significant development or a ~~historic~~ **social** event. This applies not only to great works of art but also to more modest works of the past **and present** which have acquired ~~cultural~~ **spatial** significance with the passing of time.

Article 2.
~~The conservation and restoration of monuments~~ **Transformation of buildings** must have recourse to all the sciences and techniques which can contribute to the study and safeguarding of the ~~architectural heritage~~ **resources**.

AIM

Article 3.
The intention in ~~conserving and restoring monuments~~ transforming existing **buildings** is to safeguard them no less as works of art than as ~~historical evidence~~ **untapped resources**.

~~CONSERVATION~~ **TRANSFORMATION**

Article 4.
It is essential to the ~~conservation~~ **transformation** of ~~monuments~~ **existing structures** that they be maintained on a permanent basis.

Article 5.
The ~~conservation~~ **transformation** of ~~monuments~~ **existing structures** is always facilitated by making use of them for some socially useful purpose. Such use is therefore desirable ~~but~~ **and** it ~~must not~~ **may** change the lay-out or decoration of the building. It is within ~~these~~ **economic and environmental** limits only that modifications demanded by a change of function should be envisaged and may be ~~permitted~~ **encouraged**.

Article 6.

The ~~conservation~~ **transformation** of ~~a monument~~ **an existing structure** implies ~~preserving~~ **maintaining** a setting which is not out of scale. Wherever the ~~traditional~~ setting exists, it must be kept. ~~No new~~ **Only essential** construction and demolition or modification which would alter the relations of mass and colour must be allowed.

Article 7.

~~A monument~~ **An existing structure** is inseparable from the history to which it bears witness and from the setting in which it occurs. The moving of all or part of ~~a monument~~ **an existing structure** cannot be allowed except where the safeguarding of that ~~monument~~ **existing structure** demands it ~~or where it is justified by national or international interest of paramount importance~~ **and if this is the case, it can be dismantled to be reused again**.

Article 8.

Items of sculpture, painting or decoration which form an integral part of ~~a monument~~ **an existing structure** may ~~only~~ be removed from it if this is the sole means of ~~ensuring their preservation~~ **reanimating the existing structure**.

~~RESTORATION~~ REANIMATION

Article 9.

The process of ~~restoration~~ **reanimation** is a ~~highly~~ specialized operation. Its aim is to ~~preserve~~ **invigorate** and reveal the ~~aesthetic and historic~~ **spatial** value of the ~~monument~~ **existing structure** and is based on ~~respect~~ **care** for original material **as a resource** ~~and authentic documents~~. It must ~~stop~~ **continue** at the point where conjecture begins, and in this case moreover any extra work which is ~~indispensable must be distinct from~~ **either an extension to or an insertion in** the architectural composition ~~and~~ must bear ~~a contemporary~~ **an ecological and economic** stamp. The ~~restoration~~ **reanimation** in any case must be preceded and followed by an ~~archaeological~~ **economic** and ~~historical~~ **spatial** study of the ~~monument~~ **structure**.

Article 10.

Where traditional techniques prove inadequate, the consolidation of a ~~monument~~ **structure** can be achieved by the use of any modern technique for ~~conservation and construction~~ **transformation and addition**, the efficacy of which has been shown through scientific data and proved by experience.

Article 11.

The valid contributions of all periods to the building ~~of a monument~~ must be ~~respected~~ **considered as an inventory**, since ~~unity of style is not~~ **utilising the maximum resource is** the aim of a ~~restoration~~ **transformation**. When a building includes the superimposed work of different periods, the revealing of the underlying state can ~~only~~ be justified in ~~exceptional~~ **certain** circumstances and when what is removed is of little ~~interest~~ **use and is not durable** and the ~~material~~ **volume** which is brought to light is ~~of great historical, archaeological or aesthetic value,~~ **spatially and functionally adequate** ~~and its state of preservation good enough to justify the action~~. Evaluation of the ~~importance~~ **durability** of the elements involved and the decision as to what may be destroyed cannot rest solely on the individual in charge of the work.

Article 12.

Replacements of missing parts must integrate harmoniously with the whole, but at the same time ~~must be distinguishable~~

~~from~~ **it is necessary to invigorate** the ~~original~~ **existing structure** so that ~~restoration~~ **transformation** does not falsify the ~~artistic~~ **economic** or ~~historic~~ **architectural** evidence.

Article 13.

Additions ~~cannot be~~ **are** allowed ~~except in so far as they do not detract from the interesting parts of~~ **if they are necessary for repurposing** the building, **to enliven** its ~~traditional~~ setting, **for** the balance of its composition and **to reinforce** its relation with its surroundings.

~~HISTORIC~~ **ABANDONED** SITES

Article 14.

The sites of ~~monuments~~ **structures** must be the object of special care in order to safeguard their integrity and ensure that they are cleared and presented in a seemly manner. The work of ~~conservation~~ **transformation** and ~~restoration~~ **reuse** carried out in such places should be inspired by the principles set forth in the foregoing articles.

~~EXCAVATIONS~~ **INVESTIGATIONS**

Article 15.

~~Excavations~~ **Investigations** should be carried out in

accordance with scientific standards ~~and the recommendation defining international principles to be applied in the case of archaeological excavation adopted by UNESCO in 1956.~~

~~Ruins~~ **Existing structures** must be maintained and ~~measures~~ **evidence** necessary for the ~~permanent conservation and protection~~ **transformation** of architectural features and of objects discovered must be ~~taken~~ **recorded**. Furthermore, every means must be taken to facilitate the understanding of the ~~monument~~ **structure** and to reveal it without ever ~~distorting~~ **annihilating** its meaning.

All **unnecessary** reconstruction work should however be ~~ruled out~~ **questioned** 'a priori'. ~~Only anastylosis, that is to say, the reassembling of existing but dismembered parts can be permitted.~~ The material used for integration should ~~always be recognizable~~ **be demountable** and its use should be the ~~least~~ **optimum** that will ensure the ~~conservation~~ **transformation** of a ~~monument~~ **structure** and the reinstatement of its ~~form~~ **function**.

PUBLICATION

Article 16.
In all works of ~~preservation, restoration~~ **transformation** or ~~excavation~~ **investigation**, there should always be precise documentation in the form of analytical and critical reports, illustrated with drawings and photographs. Every stage of the work of clearing, consolidation, rearrangement and integration, as well as technical and formal features identified during the course of the work, should be included **in a comprehensible manner**. This record should be placed in the archives of a public institution and made available to ~~research workers~~ **everyone**. It is recommended that the report should be published **on social media**.

Original text:
International Charter for the Conversation and Restoration of Monuments and Sites (The Venice Charter, 1964), *Scientific Journal*, ICOMOS – International Council on Monuments and Sites, 1994, icomos.org/images/DOCUMENTS/Charters/Venice_Charter_EN_2023.pdf.

⑪ Learning from

Existing structures are relational, and relations make architecture messier, more chaotic, yet stronger. Instead of ignoring these relations, we need to develop methods to learn from them. Can transforming existing structures be at the centre of the construction industry as well as architectural education and practice?

Building Chronicler

Crisis Architect

Concrete Healer

Dismantle Choreographer

Mind-Machine Interface Design I-II-III

Alternative Reality Experience Designer

Caring Studio I-II

FUTURE CURRICULUM
FUTURE PRACTICE

Artificial Intelligence in Construction I-II-III

Landscape Maintenance

Transformative Technologies I-II-III

nvironmental Impact Accountant

Structural Repair I-II

rtificial Consciousness Ethics I-II

Feasible Visualization Expert

Unheroic Design Studio I-II-III-IV

ergy Transition Consultant

Designing for Crisis I-II

Data Privacy Consultant

Building Material Recycler

Emotional Artificial Intelligence I-II-III

Dismantling Choreography I-II

Partial Recovery Architect

Virtual Identity Guardian

rowth and Stability I-II

**Extreme Engineering:
Designing for Harsh Environments I-II-III**

Climate Adaptation Strategist

Ghost Real-Estate Hunter

Inventory Recording and Visualization I-II

Healing Spaces I-II

Urban Agriculture Specialist

Reinforcement Designer

History of Relationships I-II-III

Artificial Intelligence Psychologist

Conversations with Ghosts I-II

⌣12 **Test Drive**

It is the people who keep buildings alive, and it is the buildings that keep people together. Architecture generates this symbiotic relationship. Is it possible to test with machine learning, algorithms and AI models, to break free from stereotypical perceptions of 'ugly' and 'beautiful' in order to bring the expansive stock of abandoned buildings to life again?

Here, AI figures take the place of scale drawings to
test-drive the reanimation of abandoned buildings.

⟨13⟩ Transformers

Erecting or demolishing a building is in the Hero's tale. Transforming them, is not. The Earth can no longer tolerate heroic tales, but it does need inclusive and hopeful stories of transformation.

⌣14⌣ The Pool

Before the building that represents power, there was the building that includes people. *The Carrier Bag Theory of Architecture* was derived from the transformation of an abandoned swimming pool into a public pool of listening and sharing.

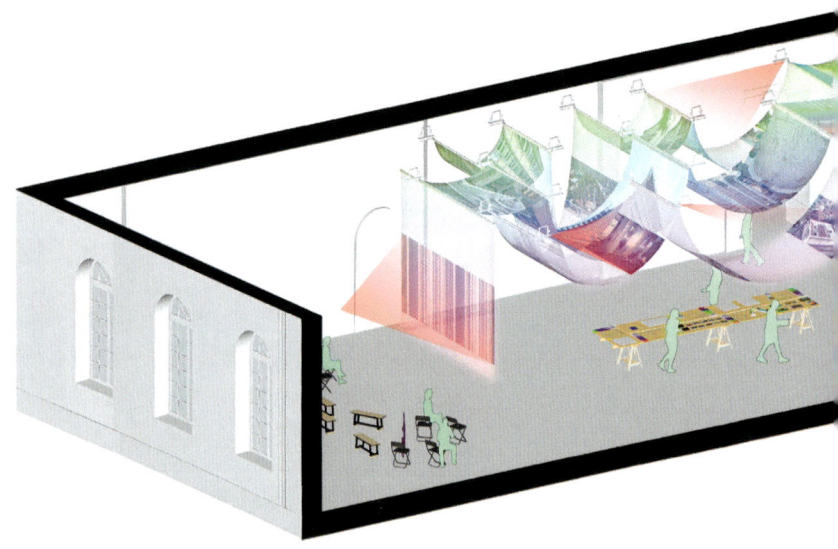

The exhibition design consists of two main parts:
The Cloud and The Workbench.

● The Cloud contains Ghost Stories such as examples of unused buildings from Türkiye.

● The Workbench is made up of fifteen tables corresponding to the fifteen articles of the 'A Manifesto for *The Carrier Bag Theory of Architecture*'. On The Workbench, questions, theories, conflicts, tools, methods and hopes are displayed.

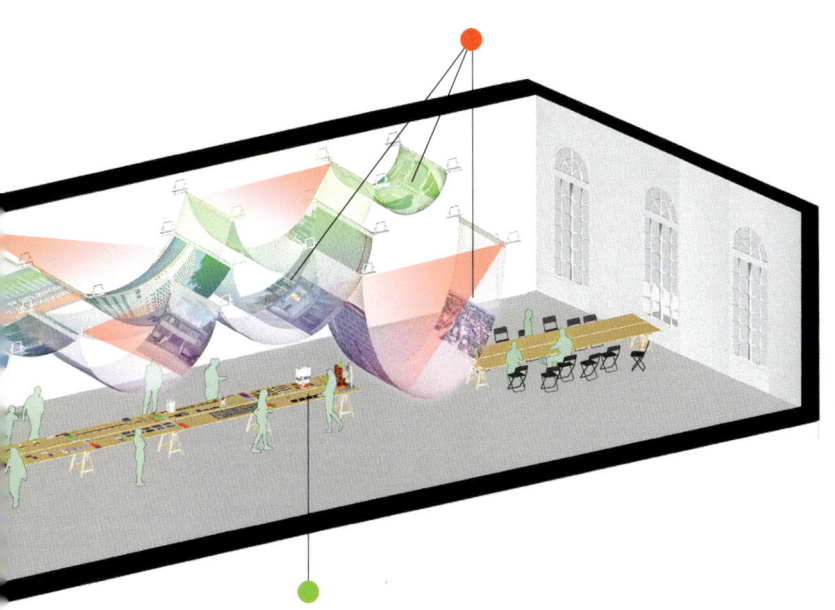

Türkiye Pavilion
18th International Architecture Exhibition – La Biennale di Venezia
20 May–26 November 2023

Ghost Stories: The Carrier Bag Theory of Architecture

PROJECT

Curators
Sevince Bayrak, Oral Göktaş

Project Team
Aysima Akın
Kevser Reyyan Doğan
Merve Akdoğan

Research Team
Mehmet Taylan Tosun
Doğu Tonkur

Research Assistants
Berke Şevketoğlu
Hatice Bahar Çoklar
Duygu Saygı

Exhibition Design
SO? Architecture and Ideas

Graphic Design
Esen Karol

Web Developer
Özhan Binici

TÜRKİYE PAVILION

Commissioner
Istanbul Foundation for Culture and Arts
(İKSV)

Selection Board
Aslı Çiçek
Prof. Dr. Ayşen Savaş
Neyran Turan
Han Tümertekin
Ertuğ Uçar

Director of İKSV Contemporary Art Projects
Bige Örer

Exhibition and Project Manager
Selen Erkal

Business Development and Project Manager
Duygu Şengünler

Managing Editor
Erim Şerifoğlu

Exhibition and Project Assistant
Aslı Esra Kocamaz

Intern
Su Güzel

İKSV

General Director
Görgün Taner

Deputy Director General
Dr. Yeşim Gürer Oymak

Deputy Director General
(Finance and Administration)
Mustafa Yegen

Assistant to General Director
Nilay Kartal

Director of Communications Group
Ayşe Bulutgil

Media Relations
Elif Ekinci, Ayşegül Öneren,
Talin Gidici, Gizem Güngör

Corporate Identity and Publications
Didem Ermiş Sezer,
Erim Şerifoğlu, Esra Kılıç,
Seren Erciyas, Sezen Özgür

Marketing
Meriç Yirmili, Canan Alper,
Emre Barış Ünel, Güneş Aydın

Sales and Business Development
Dilan Beyhan, Erim Pala,
Begüm Çavuşoğlu, Dilara Kongur

Sponsorship Programme
Zeynep Pekgöz, Zeynep Karaman

Finance and Administration
Ahmet Buruk, Başak Sucu Yıldız,
Deniz Yılmaz, Kadir Altoprak,
Özlem Can Yaşar, Berfin Doğan

Studio
Fatih Yılmaz, Kamil Kulaksız,
Sercan Bıyıklı

Production
Ali Uluç Kutal, Ulaş Bölük,
Burak Kayıkçı

Salon İKSV
Deniz Kuzuoğlu, Ufuk Şakar

Human Resources
Beste Kayacan, Yeşim Şanlı

Information Technologies
Kadir Ayyıldız, Türkay Çeler

ISTANBUL FOUNDATION FOR CULTURE AND ARTS (İKSV)

Istanbul Foundation for Culture and Arts (İKSV) is a non-profit cultural institution. Since 1973, the Foundation has continued in its efforts to enrich Istanbul's cultural and artistic life. İKSV regularly organises the Istanbul Festivals of Music, Film, Theatre and Jazz, the Istanbul Biennial, Leyla Gencer Voice Competition, autumn film week, Filmekimi and realises one-off events throughout the year. The Foundation hosts cultural and artistic events from various disciplines at its performance venue Salon İKSV, located at the Nejat Eczacıbaşı Building, and offers a creative events programme for children and youngsters at İKSV Alt Kat.

İKSV organises the Türkiye Pavilion at the International Art and Architecture Exhibitions of La Biennale di Venezia, conducts studies and drafts reports with the aim of contributing to cultural policy development, and supports artistic and cultural production through presenting awards at its festivals, commissioning works, taking part in international and local co-productions and coordinating an artist residency programme at Cité Internationale des Arts in France, as well as the annual Aydın Gün Encouragement, Talât Sait Halman Translation and Gülriz Sururi-Engin Cezzar Theatre Encouragement Awards.

İKSV has been a member of the General Assembly of the Turkish National Commission for UNESCO, since 2018.

iksv.org

ORGANISED BY

ISTANBUL FOUNDATION FOR CULTURE AND ARTS

CO-SPONSORS

WITH THE CONTRIBUTION OF

UNDER THE AUSPICES OF

REPUBLIC OF TÜRKİYE
MINISTRY OF CULTURE AND TOURISM

REPUBLIC OF TÜRKİYE
MINISTRY OF FOREIGN AFFAIRS

AIRLINE PARTNER

The Istanbul Foundation for Culture and Arts (İKSV)
would like to thank the following individuals and institutions for their
contribution towards securing a long-term venue
for the Türkiye Pavilion for the period 2014–2034.

AKBANK

MEHVEŞ-DALINÇ ARIBURNU

BERRAK-NEZİH BARUT

ALİ RAİF DİNÇKÖK

VUSLAT DOĞAN SABANCI & ALİ SABANCI

FÜSUN-FARUK ECZACIBAŞI

OYA-BÜLENT ECZACIBAŞI

NESRİN ESİRTGEN

ETİ GIDA SAN. VE TİC. AŞ

GARANTİ BBVA

AHU-CAN HAS

ÖNER KOCABEYOĞLU

MAÇAKIZI

TANSA MERMERCİ EKŞİOĞLU

SAHA ASSOCIATION

RANA-EROL TABANCA

TAHA TATLICI

SİNAN TARA

VEHBİ KOÇ FOUNDATION

ZAFER YILDIRIM

YILDIZ HOLDİNG AŞ

*Acknowledging their kind contributions
towards the realisation of the project:*

Ankara Metropolitan Municipality
Ara Güler Archives
    and Research Center
Ara Güler Museum
Benice Logistics
Bolton & Quinn
Boston Dynamics
DHA
General Consulate of Italy
    in Istanbul
Istanbul Metropolitan Municipality
Istanbul Planning Agency (IPA)
Italian Cultural Institute
KAF Kolektif
Kahramanmaraş Chamber
    of Architects
MEF University Faculty of Arts
    Design and Architecture
Mersin Metropolitan Municipality
We Exhibit

Burak Abaşlıoğlu,
Tamer Abaşlıoğlu, Gökhan Açıksarı,
Artin Aharon, Elif Akman,
Büke Akşehirli, Canan Arslantaş,
Göksu Aydoğan, Ceylin Başer,
İdil Bayar, Leyla Bayrı,
Elena Clemente, Bengisu Çağlayan,
Nur Banu Çelik, Burçin Çevik,
Ekin Çuhadar, Silvia Dalloca,
Cemal Emden, Baran Ertürk,
Melis Erüstün Bezmez,
İpek Gençler, Burak Güç,
İrem Gülbaş Dinek,
Ceren Güler, Volkan Gültekin,
Yunus Emre Kaçamaz,
Oktay Kargül, Şerif Kocaman,
Çağrı Köseyener, Ümit Mesci,
Gamze Özbaş, Onur Öztürk,
Irene Pastorini, Jane Quinn,
Luca Racchini, Micol Saleri,
Özlem Serdar, Zeynep Seyhun,
Emre Seymenoğlu,
Gözde Selenay Şahin, Özkan Şener,
Maria Tasca, Erinç Tepetaş,
Umut Barış Yıldırım

Supporting Tulip Card Members

Selin Açık
Ebru Dildar Edin
Levent Keser
Gülfem Köseoğlu
Emine Öz
Oğuz Sönmez
Oluş Sönmez
Elvan Tuğsuz Güven

*A thank-you note
from Sevince and Oral:*

We are grateful to our project and
research team for collaborating
us in this project and Aysima Akın,
Reyyan Doğan and Merve Akdoğan
for their endless effort. We want
to thank Arzu Erdem, Mark West,
Onur Uygun and Evren Uzer for
their contributions to our manifesto,
Şebnem Yücel for reading the first
draft and sharing her constructive
comments, Yaniv Berman,
Philippe Ruault, Emine Nur Uzdil
for their photos, Ensar Yılmaz,
Deniz Ova, Arda İnceoğlu and
Ali Köseoğlu for their support,
Cem Dinlenmiş for his illustration,
İKSV and ListLAB for sharing
our passion about this book.
We are grateful to Denise Scott
Brown who shared her thoughts
about our theory which encouraged
us. Special thanks to Esen Karol
for giving us the idea of making this
book, and it was a real privilege to
have her in our team. We would like
to thank everyone who contributed
to our open call for *Ghost Stories*,
for enriching this discussion
about the future of our cities.

*Thank you for participating in our open call
to document abandoned buildings across Türkiye.*

Through e-mail Ahmet Gökhan Demirer, Ahmet Turan Köksal, Alp Emre Çelik, Alperen Beyan, Altuğ Çırakoğlu, Aslı Felah, Aybüke Çakmak, Aysel Yılmaz, Ayşe Gülsevin Tamer & Vecdi Tamer, Ayşe Karakoç, Ayşe Sena Gürcan, Ayşegül Çetinkaya, Ayşegül Sezer, Ayşegül Yüksel, Bahar Türkay, Bahriye Kabadayı Dal, Behçet Teuman, Behiye Işın Haksal, Belis Öztürk, Berfin Coşkuner, Berfin Güzel, Berin Gür, Berkan Çelik, Berkay Edis, Beyhan Güneş, Bilal İmren, Buket Ergün Kocaili, Burak Altınışık, Burak Dikilitaş, Burcu Yasemin Türkay, Buse Damla Eray, Bünyamin Tan, Büşra Nur Tatlı, Cemile Hacıferhatoğlu, Ceren Hamiloğlu, Ceyda Tahan, Çiğdem Çavdaroğlu, Demet Dursun, Didem Avincan, Didem Yavuz, Dilan Durusoy, Dilara Atalay, Duru Tanır, Ebru Şahinkaya & Aytaç Taşkın, Ece İrem Tuncer, Ecem Kırtaş, Eda Özgener, Edanur İmanlı, Elif Bekar, Elif Birdoğan, Elif Kır Cullen, Elizhan Tuğana Eren, Emin Altan, Emine Meltem Serdar, Erhan Muratoğlu, Esin Bölükbaş Dayı & Hilal Tuğba Örmecioğlu, Evrim Özsoy, Ezgi Hamzaçebi, Ferya Alkan, Ferzan Müsellim, Feyza Çınar, Filiz Çelebi, Filiz Ünsal, Funda Pehlivan Eker, Funda Uz, Gökhan Kocamanoğlu, Gözde Özder, Gül Bilgin, Gülin Erden, Gülnihal Barbarosoğlu, Gürkan Okumuş, H. Yiğit Ceylan, Hande Savaş, Herkes İçin Mimarlık Derneği, Işık Özdal, İbrahim Kaymaz, İlker Aksoy, İrem Savcı, İris Eryılmaz, Kıvılcım Göksu Toprak, Mediha Didem Türemen, Mehmet Eray Atay, Mehmet Sait Aktay, Mehmet Taylan Tosun, Melda Osmanoğlu, Melike Yakarer, Melis Akay, Meltem Şahin, Merve Altunel, Merve Köseoğlu, Merve Osal, Metehan Özcan, Münire Sağat, Nevzat Sayın, Nilay Akbaytürk, Nisa Yazıcı, Nur Güzeldere, Nur Melis Turhan, Nurdan Özgür, Orçun Karamustafa, Osman Faruk Akkum, Osman Süreyya Kocabaş, Ömer Efe Göktekin, Ömer Faruk Doğan, Özge Öztürk, Özge Yağcı, Özlem Dengiz & Cem Cüneyt Uğur, Özlem Yalım, Öznur Aktaş, Pelin Kayhan, Pelin Özdemir, Renan Teuman, Rümeysa Arslan, Sakine Çil, Samim Magriso, Seda Subaşı, Selen Erkal, Sena Özfiliz, Simge Büyükbaş, Sinan Güldal, Sinan Uçarsu, Sinem Avcı Koyunsev, Şizen Türkal, Tuba Nil Akçaylı, Tuğba Özçelik Günay, Tuğçe Diler, Tuna Pektaş, Ümit Alptekin, Yalın Zabun, Yunus Emre Turgut, Yusuf Pinhas, Zeynep Ayaşlıgil, Zeynep Demirhan, Zeynep Hazal Taş Fazlı

Through Instagram Ali Rıza Bayrak, Aliye Erol, @ankaraapartmanlari, @artik.mimar, Aşkın Ercan, Aydın Eren Dinçer, Barış Çakmakçı, @bberivanguzel, Begüm Aksay Savçın, Berkan Çelik Mimarlık, @biaralikkultursanat, Bora Eşiz, Can Çilek, Duygu Tüntaş, @edanrkilic, Elif Kartal, Elif Sidar Okdemir, Ezgi Yılmaz Arz, Fatma Gültekin, Fatih Gökmen, @felanikli, @gilsah, @_gisay, @gokcealgan, Gülistan Kenanoğlu, Havva Yılmaz, @harabedelisi, İbrahim Akgün, İlayda Şahin, @itulumimart, @jupiter_s_groove_stain, @laisphotog, @leylaheps, Mehmet Berk Yaltırık, Meral Ağar, Mert Başbuğ, Mert Karakurt, Merve İpek, Mehmet Atılgan, Murat Çetinkaya, @mustrekl, @myfotografisleri, Naz Eraslan, Onur Uygun, @rotaninrehberi, @sagun65, Yeşim Levent – Bradley, Sıla Kara, @simci.s.works, @sistersinbw, Yasemin Karakaya, @yikildilar

The publisher would like to thank all those who have kindly given their permission for the reproduction of material for this book. Every effort has been made to obtain permission to reproduce the images. However, as is standard editorial policy, the publisher is at the disposal of copyright holders and undertakes to correct any omissions or errors in future editions.

All images are courtesy of

Ghost Stories:
The Carrier Bag Theory
of Architecture
Sevince Bayrak, Oral Göktaş

This book is co-published
by the Istanbul Foundation
for Culture and Arts (İKSV)
and ListLab on the occasion
of the exhibition:

Ghost Stories:
The Carrier Bag Theory
of Architecture
Türkiye Pavilion
18th International
Architecture Exhibition
La Biennale di Venezia

20 May–26 November 2023

Managing Editor
Erim Şerifoğlu

Text
Sevince Bayrak

Copy Editing
Melissa Larner
Aaron Juneau (A Manifesto for
The Carrier Bag Theory of Architecture)

Graphic Design
Esen Karol

Publication Assistant
Kevser Reyyan Doğan

Printed and bound in Turkey by
Ofset Yapımevi, Istanbul, 2023

Listlab Editorial Director
Alessandro Martinelli
asma.meetarch (IG)

Sales, Marketing and Distribution
Jacopo Marcomeni
distribution@listlab.eu
listlab.eu/en/distribuzione

ISBN 978-883-2080-78-0

Istanbul Foundation for Culture and Arts
Nejat Eczacıbaşı Binası
Sadi Konuralp Caddesi No: 5
34433 Şişhane, Istanbul, Turkey
iksv.org

LISTLAB

List Laboratorio
Internazionale Editoriale S.r.l.
c/ Llull, 47 6-8
08005 Barcelona, Spain
listlab.eu

ListLab was established in 2007 and has
elaborated on the idea of an international editorial
laboratory with a multidisciplinary approach
to architecture, planning, arts, photography,
and design. List Group, found in 2021, aims at
creating networks and promoting debates and
cultural exchange, but also organize events
from which new knowledge about architecture,
cities, and landscape can develop. Today,
List Group is composed of **ListLab**, the publishing
house, **Blacklist**, the graphic design studio,
Instaura, the informational weblog, and
Us/Them/Yours, a creative agency that aims
at a multimedia approach to information.